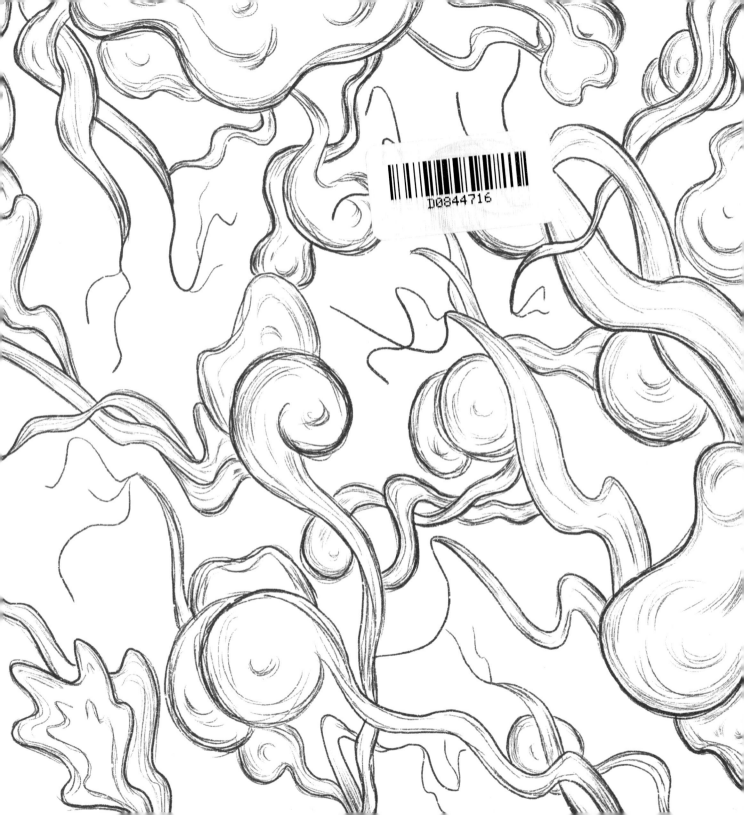

FEAR NOT!

How to face your fear and anxiety head-on

Christina Furnival

ILLUSTRATED BY Katie Dwyer

FEAR NOT!
Copyright © 2022 by Christina Furnival

Published by:
PESI Publishing, Inc.
3839 White Ave
Eau Claire, WI 54703

Illustrations: Katie Dwyer
Cover: Katie Dwyer
Layout: Katie Dwyer, Amy Rubenzer

9781683734833 (print)
9781683734840 (ePUB)
9781683734857 (ePDF)
9781683734901 (KPF)

PESI Publishing
pesipublishing.com

Dedication

To my fabulous, fun, and impossibly posh in-laws, Angela and David. This book is for you. You make me feel like such a cherished member of the family, helping to minimize any fears and anxieties I could have.

If you're reading this book, then you might be like me,
with some fears and some worries that won't let you be.

We are in this together, I want you to know.
All kids (grown-ups too!) have these thoughts come and go.

Yes, grown-ups have fears! Can't believe it? It's true!
Worries bother us **all**—not just me, not just you.

I'll tell you the story of beating my fears,
so listen up now 'cause I need you all ears!

There were times in my life when I had a big fear.

It was constantly with me; it always felt near.

WHAT DIDN'T WORK

So what did I do when fear entered my head?
I'll tell you what **didn't** work, then I'll tell you what **did.**

I kept it a secret,
which felt like protection,
but I was alone,
without help or connection.

I hoped that if I could pretend it was gone,
that it simply would leave me alone and move on.

So I tried to ignore it,
to push it away,
but this didn't work
and it felt here to stay.

It took over my focus,
and *that* didn't fix it.
It was all I could think of,
I just couldn't nix it.

Then one windy day when I noticed the breeze,
I started to feel that my mind was at ease.

All my senses woke up as the air passed me by.

I was touching and feeling the swirls of the sky.

Then my smell, taste, and sight were also turned on,
and most of all sound, with a lovely bird's song.

More aware of my surroundings,
something wonderful shifted.

As I focused on senses, my fear. . . it just lifted!

As my worries kept fading,
I was learning (with pride!)
there were things I could do
to make *fear* want to hide.

WHAT DID WORK

I will share with you now my step-by-step plan
so that you, too, can do it—I know that you can!

First notice, accept, and acknowledge the fear.
Now describe it out loud, in a voice strong and clear.

'Cause by voicing our thoughts we strip fear of its power.
We strengthen ourselves and then **fear** starts to cower.

STEP 2

And now, let's remember:
The feeling will pass!
It will not hang around
because feelings don't last.

Our nice feelings and yuck ones
all act just the same—
they come for a while,
then they go on their way!

This last step is to pick out
our favorite new tool
to help cope and to manage—
to regain our cool.

Slow deep breathing's a tool
to take charge of our mind,
soothing heads, hearts, and tummies,
leaving fears far behind.

Tools could also be writing
or sipping a drink,

maybe drawing, or puzzling, or *sleeping a wink.*

The more that I practiced, the better I got
at using my tools, telling fear:

You can practice these steps just like I did before.
I know you can do it and shout out:

Watch your confidence **grow**, and big worries shrink **small**,
as you take on your fears with these steps, tools, and all.

And although there are times
when the fear will creep in,
you are now strong and skilled,
and you've learned how to win.

Fears aren't so scary if
we don't let them be.
When we face them head-on,
we can bravely be free.

Note to Parents and Professionals

This story in the *Capable Kiddos* series involves the topics of fear, worry, and anxiety. Although you'll notice that the word "fear" is used most frequently throughout this story, it is representative of anxious thoughts and anxiety as well.

All children will develop fears and worries, often feeling powerless to handle them. When children don't have the skills to cope, their worry can grow bigger, and their confidence can plummet, sometimes leading to clinical depression and anxiety disorders. As parents, teachers, and counselors, we can utilize this story to support our children to grow in mindfulness, develop a toolbox of coping skills, and effectively and confidently manage their fear and anxiety.

Conversation Starters and Discussion Questions

- **What are fear and anxiety?**

  Fear and anxiety are natural and protective emotions in response to danger. Fear is often about a known danger that is about to happen or is already happening, whereas anxiety is often about an unknown danger or something that might happen in the future.

- **What are some fears or worries that you and others have?**

  Share honestly with your trusted adult. I bet they have some fears and anxieties they can share with you too!

- **Who experiences fear and anxiety?**

  Everyone! There is not a single person who doesn't have fears and anxieties from time to time. You are not alone in what you're thinking and feeling.

- **When can fears or worries be helpful? When can they become a concern?**

  Fear and anxiety can help keep us safe by letting us know when something is dangerous or risky. We can listen to the helpful messages fear and anxiety tell us in order to make wise and safe choices.

  Both fear and anxiety are not helpful when they become overactive. This is when our body is acting as if there is danger, even where there is none. We may have the "what ifs" and spend a lot of our time and energy worrying about things that may never happen. Overactive fear and anxiety can lead us to avoid things and miss out on activities or events.

- **What are coping skills?**

Coping skills are actions to help yourself. You use coping skills to manage or regulate your emotions and regain a state of calm. There are so many options of coping skills to choose from, such as doing a puzzle, telling yourself happy things, picturing your favorite place, moving your body in a fun or silly way, writing down your thoughts, or talking to a friend—the list goes on! The more types of coping skills you try, the more you learn which ones work best for you. Certain coping skills will work better for different moods or situations. One coping skill that almost always helps is mindfully taking slow, deep breaths, breathing in through your nose, holding your breath, and breathing out slowly through your mouth.

- **What is mindfulness?**

Mindfulness means to intentionally focus your attention to the present moment, your senses, and your surroundings. It is a fabulous tool for your coping skills toolbox because it can help you calm your body, and it takes your focus away from your fears and anxieties.

- **What are the three steps in the book to cope with anxiety and fear?**

The three steps are to:

1. *Notice, accept, acknowledge, and voice your fear.* Tell a trusted adult what you're thinking and feeling. You may think that speaking about your scary thoughts out loud will make you feel even more scared, but in reality, you'll feel better!

2. *Remember that the fear or anxiety will not be with you forever.* Feelings are like waves in the ocean—they come and go! When you remember this, you are better able to tolerate the discomfort of fear and anxiety whenever they pop up because you know they will leave soon.

3. *Use mindfulness and coping skills to calm your body and mind.* You have the power to help yourself by being mindful and by using coping skills that make you feel better.

- **What coping skills help you the most when you're scared or worried? Which ones can you do, and which ones can your parents or other trusted adults do for or with you?**

You can help yourself by using mindfulness and coping skills, and if you need extra support (which we all do sometimes!), then you can ask your trusted adults to help you. Sometimes a hug and some reassurance are enough. Other times you may want to do deep breathing along with them.

About the Author

Christina Furnival, MS, LPCC, is a wife, mother of two, writer, author, and licensed mental health therapist. With over a decade of experience in the field, she is passionate about helping parents and children grow their skill sets, overcome challenges, and gain confidence to live happy, fulfilling lives.

Her meaningful stories in the *Capable Kiddos* series serve as entertaining and enlightening resources to empower children and to make them feel capable of managing tough situations and their accompanying emotions. Visit her at ChristinaFurnival.com and on Instagram @CapableKiddosBooks.

About the Illustrator

Katie Dwyer is a children's book illustrator living in the magical woods of Asheville, North Carolina, with her husband and three wildlings. She loves illustrating stories that teach valuable lessons while adding a twist of whimsical charm. When she's not drawing or painting in her studio, she can be found drinking iced matcha lattes with her nose in a book or watching a good movie. Visit her at katiedwyerillustrations.com or on Instagram @katiedwyer.illustrations.

Also in the *Capable Kiddos Series*

CAPABLE KIDDOS SERIES